MIGHTY MACHINES IN ACTION

Garbage Trucks

by Thomas K. Adamson

BELLWETHER MEDIA • MINNEAPOLIS, MN

Note to Librarians, Teachers, and Parents:

Blastoff! Readers are carefully developed by literacy experts and combine standards-based content with developmentally appropriate text.

Level 1 provides the most support through repetition of high-frequency words, light text, predictable sentence patterns, and strong visual support.

Level 2 offers early readers a bit more challenge through varied simple sentences, increased text load, and less repetition of high-frequency words.

Level 3 advances early-fluent readers toward fluency through increased text and concept load, less reliance on visuals, longer sentences, and more literary language.

Level 4 builds reading stamina by providing more text per page, increased use of punctuation, greater variation in sentence patterns, and increasingly challenging vocabulary.

Level 5 encourages children to move from "learning to read" to "reading to learn" by providing even more text, varied writing styles, and less familiar topics.

Whichever book is right for your reader, Blastoff! Readers are the perfect books to build confidence and encourage a love of reading that will last a lifetime!

This edition first published in 2017 by Bellwether Media, Inc.

No part of this publication may be reproduced in whole or in part without written permission of the publisher. For information regarding permission, write to Bellwether Media, Inc., Attention: Permissions Department, 5357 Penn Avenue South, Minneapolis, MN 55419.

Library of Congress Cataloging-in-Publication Data

Names: Adamson, Thomas K., 1970- author.
Title: Garbage Trucks / by Thomas K. Adamson.
Description: Minneapolis, MN : Bellwether Media, Inc., 2017. | Series: Blastoff! Readers. Mighty Machines in Action |
   Audience: Ages 5-8. | Audience: K to grade 3. | Includes bibliographical references and index.
Identifiers: LCCN 2016034481 (print) | LCCN 2016035175 (ebook) | ISBN 9781626176058
   (hardcover : alk. paper) | ISBN 9781681033358 (ebook)
Subjects: LCSH: Refuse collection vehicles–Juvenile literature.
Classification: LCC TD792 .A33 2017 (print) | LCC TD792 (ebook) | DDC 628.4/420284–dc23
LC record available at https://lccn.loc.gov/2016034481

Editor: Christina Leighton   Designer: Steve Porter

Printed in the United States of America, North Mankato, MN.

Table of
Contents

TRASH SMASH

A garbage truck stops at a house. Its robotic arm reaches out and grabs a garbage can.

robotic arm →

The arm lifts the can and
tips it upside down.

Clunk! Bang! Trash **tumbles** into the garbage truck.

6

The arm sets the garbage can down. Then the truck **rumbles** to the next house!

TRUCKLOADS OF TRASH

landfill

Garbage trucks collect trash.
They carry the trash to **landfills**.

Some trucks pick up **recycled** items. They carry the items to recycling centers.

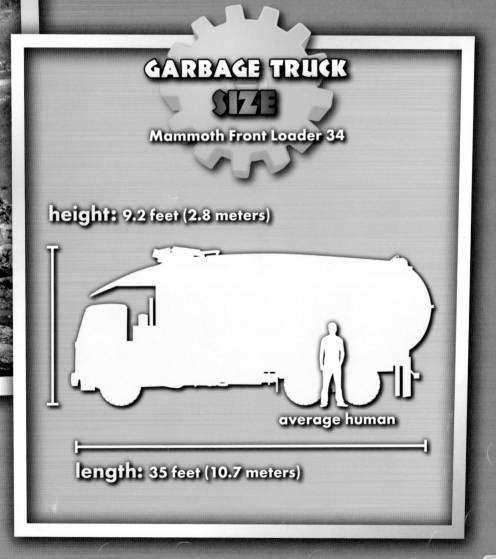

GARBAGE TRUCK
SIZE
Mammoth Front Loader 34

height: 9.2 feet (2.8 meters)

average human

length: 35 feet (10.7 meters)

Many garbage trucks
pick up trash from homes.

MACHINE PROFILE
McNEILUS® M5 REAR LOADER

length: 17.3 feet (5.3 meters)

height: 6.7 feet (2 meters)

hopper: 16 seconds to crush garbage

dumpster →

Others go to businesses, schools, and apartments. They use big forks to lift **dumpsters**.

TIRES, HOPPERS, AND BLADES

All garbage trucks have large tires to support heavy loads.

tire

Garbage trucks also have
loud, powerful engines.

Garbage trucks have **hoppers**. They can hold tons of weight.

hopper

packer blade

Most hoppers have **packer blades**. These crush trash to make more room.

Some garbage trucks open from the back. Workers get out of the truck.

They may empty garbage cans themselves. Others line cans up with the truck's lifting arm.

grapple

Other trucks are controlled from the inside. A robotic arm lifts the garbage can.

Some trucks have **grapples** to pick up large items.

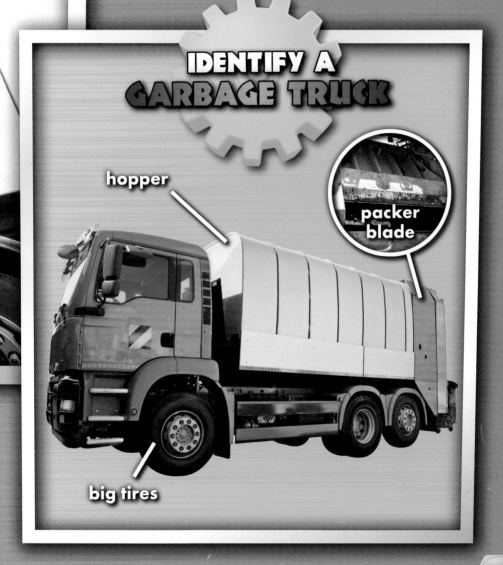

IDENTIFY A
GARBAGE TRUCK

hopper

packer blade

big tires

Garbage trucks do dirty work.
They deal with loads of trash.

These mighty trucks help keep neighborhoods and cities clean!

Glossary

dumpsters—large bins that hold trash

grapples—large metal jaws that can pick up heavy objects

hoppers—the parts of garbage trucks that hold trash

landfills—areas where garbage and other materials are taken

packer blades—metal blades that crush trash inside garbage trucks to make more room

recycled—sorted to make used items into new ones

rumbles—makes a low sound while moving

tumbles—falls and rolls suddenly

To Learn More

AT THE LIBRARY

Carr, Aaron. *Garbage Trucks*. New York, N.Y.: AV2 by Weigl, 2016.

Meister, Cari. *Garbage Trucks*. Minneapolis, Minn.: Jump!, 2014.

Murray, Julie. *Garbage Trucks*. Minneapolis, Minn.: ABDO Kids, 2016.

ON THE WEB

Learning more about garbage trucks is as easy as 1, 2, 3.

1. Go to www.factsurfer.com.

2. Enter "garbage trucks" into the search box.

3. Click the "Surf" button and you will see a list of related web sites.

With factsurfer.com, finding more information is just a click away.

Index

The images in this book are reproduced through the courtesy of: Jennifer Pitiquen, front cover; LABeats, pp. 4-5; Johnny Habell, pp. 5, 10-11; JohnnyH5, pp. 6-7; Samir Delic, pp. 8-9; McNeilus, p. 10; Dmitry Kalinovsky, p. 12; Taina Sohlman, p. 13; vadim kozlovsky, p. 14; KPG_Payless, pp. 14-15; 360b, pp. 16-17; Carolina K. Smith MD, p. 17; vm, pp. 18-19; mladn61, p. 19 (truck); tzahiV, p. 19 (packing blade); martin berry/ Alamy, pp. 20-21.